MEMOIRS

of

William Lawson Crouse

March 2012

* A small child growing up during The Great Depression
* A teenager during WWII
* As a Navy enlisted man experiencing the Korean War in Airgroup #2 and #19 with task force #77

WILLIAM L. CROUSE

ISBN 978-1-64416-843-1 (paperback)
ISBN 978-1-64416-844-8 (digital)

Christian Faith Publishing, Inc.
832 Park Avenue
Meadville, PA 16335
www.christianfaithpublishing.com

Printed in the United States of America

CHAPTER 1

Growing Up in the Great Depression and WWII

I was born in Syracuse, New York, at Memorial Hospital on August 23, 1928. Did my father need the expense of a new baby?

Growing up, I attended public elementary school located four blocks from my house. No school buses then, so I had to walk in all weather. My mother bought me knickers (knee highs) and boots called high tops (eight to ten inches high). The top of the boot had a sheath to carry a pocket knife. We wore caps (no baseball caps then). I was in my glory with this outfit, plus I carried marbles in my pocket. To this day, I still carry a pocket knife. Used it once to gut out a deer that fell dead.

My father, my uncle, and my grandfather worked in the family grocery store from 7:00 AM to 11:00 PM. In the Depression, unemployment in the cities was about 20 percent. In rural areas of New York, it was 30 percent. Farmers were better off if they had a garden, meat, and milk. My family was living on the first floor of a two-family house owned by my grandfather (I think the rent was forgiven). Probably groceries came from grandfather's store. It became clear that the grocery store would not support three families, so my father left to find work. He found some part-time work but was mostly unemployed for one year. He finally went to work for the WPA (Works Progress Administration). This was a government supported program to provide jobs for men to work on infrastructure projects such as roads, sewers, etc.

My mother would buy two or three live chickens. The boys' job was to kill them. Grab bird by the feet, put head on chopping block, and using a sharp ax, cut off head. Let bird run sometimes twenty to forty feet. Blood all over, including us. Murderers! Where is PETA when we need them? Boil water in bucket; dip whole bird in hot water. Pluck feathers off bird, easy now. Let bird cool off and gut bird. Save liver for the cat. Put in icebox (no refrigerators or freezers).

Mother prepared meal for all. Sunday was a feast: chickens (roasted), mashed potatoes, two vegetables, plus rolls. Monday, still not bad . . . lots of leftovers. Tuesday, looks more like chicken soup. Wednesday and Thursday, hard to find any chicken . . . rice now added to mixture or a few potatoes. Friday, fish (creamed tuna). Saturday, a surprise? Mother was great at baking bread, rolls, pies, cookies . . . all natural, no box stuff.

Fortunately, I have always had money. Father, if he had any money, would give a small allowance, like five cents. However, when I was twelve or thirteen years old, I started working in the family grocery store. The store had a fountain and I was a "soda jerk." Pay was fifteen cents per hour. Worked mostly in the summer and weekends in the rest of the year. At the same time, during the winter months, I contracted with three homes to shovel snow for fifty cents per week. If a twenty-four-inch snow fell, it would hurt my back. If no snow fell, I would still collect $1.50 per week. I was rich!

My father sent me to private school, CBA (Christian Brothers Academy) in Syracuse. Dad gave me ten cents per day to take the trolley or bus to school two miles away. However, if I walked three blocks to the north, the bus there would give me a transfer to ride another bus three blocks to the south. Net savings twenty-five cents per week. Sometimes, if the weather was warm, I would walk two miles home.

My grandfather (now retired) purchased an old rural house as a family camp a couple of miles from Oneida Lake in Cleveland, NY. This became the summer gathering place for all the relatives. The old folks had a garden for fresh vegetables. We could buy meat, chicken, eggs, milk from farmers. These meals were the best ever eaten. It was all fresh.

The boys in the family had BB guns, slingshots, and fireworks. The Fourth of July was a "blast." We put cherry bombs under empty cans and they shot forty feet in the air. If you put a cherry bomb in the nearby stream, it would kill the fish. *How to catch a fish without rod and reel.* One time I used a BB gun to shoot a cow in the field nearby. I am now confessing that I did the deed. Conclusion: The cow really does jump over the moon!

The camp had no electricity, so oil lamps were the only source of light. We learned to play cards (pinochle). My Irish uncle would accuse my old German great-aunts of cheating at cards. The two great-aunts were closest to angels, but when they were wrongly accused, they had a temper.

My two uncles were golfers. They practiced hitting balls into the cow field in back of the family camp. After hitting about twenty-five balls, each boy's job was to fetch the balls. At least four or five would end up in fresh cow flop. How to retrieve balls from pile of poop? Take a stick and remove ball from bad stuff. Roll in grass until it looks clean. Smell to see if the ball *is* clean. Pick up with a handkerchief. Dump with other balls. Problem: golfers wanted same number of balls returned. Mothers, "What happened to your handkerchief?"

"I lost it."

In the late 1940s, a battery-powered TRF (tuned radio frequency) radio was brought to camp. On the weekends, we like to listen to football games. You guessed it—Notre Dame. The radio had about eight dials and would squeak and fade. For my birthday, my father bought me a crystal set plus headset and long metal antenna. Would listen to *The Shadow* and *Sherlock Holmes.* The "Hound of the Baskervilles" still sends a shiver up my spine. The fidelity of the crystal set was perfect. Was supposed to not listen after eight o'clock. "I'm just sleeping with head set on."

"Okay."

Grandfather passed on and uncle drafted for WWII. Family store now run by father. Rationing was instituted on gas, clothing, food products, and meat. We all had ration cards, even babies. No ration stamps, no food. Wholesale grocers required stamps or no sale. Our gas rationing card was for five gallons per week. Gas price was eighteen cents per gallon. Cigarettes were scarce, but not rationed. Had to hide cigarettes below checkout counter. Had to learn how to lie with a straight face. Good customers would get some, others . . . no chance. Cigarettes cost fifteen cents per pack, but we sold them for a penny each. Profit five cents per pack.

When low or out of beer, we would hook up old trailer and hit the breweries. If possible pick up fifteen to twenty cases and smuggle them in to back door of store. Put some on ice and rest go to back room . . . most for favorite customers. "Do you have beer?"

"No, no, no." Had to lie again! God help me!

During WWII, things had to change. All city lights were blacked out. All house and store lights were not to be visible. My father was a fire warden, and his area was four blocks. If lights were visible, he turned people in to authorities if warning was not adhered to.

All metals were saved for the war effort. "Rag men" pushed carts down Main Street. They paid cash for rags, papers, tires, etc. One hundred pounds of papers shot up to $1 per load. Boy Scouts would collect door-to-door for valuable items. Civil Defense would demonstrate how to put out an incendiary after lighting one in our attic. A large tub of sand was kept in the attic. Using a regular lighted bomb, it was placed in the sand with tongs and covered with sand, therefore smothering the bomb. Never use water! Returning veterans were treated like heroes.

Ice men delivered ice to the icebox each day, if needed. Had to put two feet by two feet large card in front window with "25," "50," "75," "100" on each horizontal surface. If "50" was on top, he would pick up fifty-pound chunk and put it in top of icebox. One hundred pounds was no problem. He would even haul it upstairs to second floor for cousin's icebox. Ice man had a leather covering on his right shoulder to keep ice water from dripping on clothes.

During WWII, coal was scarce as were men to work. An order of coal would be dropped off at curb-side on street level. Problem: to get coal up a small hill to house and dump it in coal chute and into the cellar. Father was now working twelve to sixteen hours per day. Guess who was elected to move coal. "Black Gold"—if left out people would steal it. In the cellar was a small wood stove to heat water. Only used when needed. Fire out = cold water bath.

Teenagers had to work to survive. In those days, bank representatives would go to elementary school and encourage students to start saving accounts. Pennies or nickels would start. I still try to save something each pay day.

Had to walk two miles to junior high school. No train or bus rides then.

In 1945, I visited Tupper Lake, NY, with the Boy Scouts. We rented a camp at Little Wolf. Went fishing at Underwood Bridge (junction between Raquette Pond and Raquette River). Hooked a large northern pike, but lost the fish; line broke. Went into Tupper Lake one night. A whistle blew at nine o'clock. All kids sixteen and under had to be off the street. Would this work today?

Father rigged a shooting gallery in our basement. Using twenty-two shorts, we would shoot very often. One night, I loaded the gun and pointed it up. Little brother pulled the trigger. Mother was seated above at dining room table. The bullet went through the floor, hitting table. Mother yelled, "Stop it! You almost shot me."

"The baby did it." A close one!

As a youth, I liked to build model airplanes from kits. Most were powered by rubber bands. My problem was, I liked to fly them off high perches and set them on fire or blow them up with fireworks. An expensive hobby. Watching them crash drew a crowd of other misfits. Later in life, I saw the real thing while serving on many aircraft carriers. For a Boy Scout merit badge, I raised carrier pigeons. To keep my birds pure, had to "whack off" impure birds. It's called euthanasia. Don't tell PETA.

Father bought me a "bang site" cannon. Calcium carbide added to water makes an explosive gas (acetylene). When fired, the report was louder than today's deer rifles. Neighbors complained. My hearing has never been the same.

Modern technology finally came to the camp. Father put in a new toilet with septic tank. What to do with the old two-holer outhouse plus Sears catalogs used to wipe? Let's burn it. Okay. Friends and neighbors gathered and outhouse was torched. People did Indian dance until it was ashes. No arson then.

At camp, kids played Monopoly sometimes for three or four days. Some days, we should read the rules.

Old great-aunts decided to paper the walls in their bedroom. They mixed flour and water to make paste. The next spring, when camp opened, the mice had eaten the new paper off the walls as far as they could reach. Try again.

Two Irish uncles into the sauce came back to camp, but the doors were locked. They found an open window, crawled inside, and laid down on the bed just below the window. Unfortunately the bed was already occupied by one of my old maiden aunts. She woke up screaming that she was being attacked. The whole camp was aroused. Back then, you could shoot intruders. Lucky uncles!

Before the age of reason "us boys" started smoking. We made corn cob pipes from kitchen leftovers. Put into pipes dried leaves, corn silk, old cigarette butts, and almost anything else that would burn. Terrible odor. Mother, "I smell smoke."

"It's okay. Just lighting small stove for hot water. You know how I like to be clean."

CHAPTER 2

Snippets from the Past

1. I was locked in the basement of St. Agnes Church in Lake Placid after a meeting.
2. When in the service (US Navy) crossed the Pacific Ocean six times.
3. Had an APB issued for stealing a car in San Francisco while attending a cousin's wedding. The parking garage gave us the wrong car.
4. Had to relearn how to walk at age twelve due to a heart malfunction. Was in bed three months; after, no sports.
5. Made seventeen Adirondack guide boats. One made at Mallow Castle in Ireland.
6. Served on six US aircraft carriers: USS *Midway*, USS *Boxer*, USS *Valley Forge*, USS *Philippine Sea*, USS *Bon Homme Richard*, and USS *Princeton*.
7. As of this year, 2012, have been in Big Simond Hunting Club for fifty-four years.
8. Injured in doctor's office on August 9, 2011. Nurse did not hit me!
9. Gave artificial respiration twice. First, at Tupper Lake High School. Male fell while running around school track. The second was while driving with son to Childwold, NY, we

came upon an accident where car was T-boned. Girl was in correct position for CPR, but both people died.

10. Been in Ireland three times.

11. Been sober for twenty-eight years.

12. Have twelve to twenty-two grandchildren and great-grandkids. Can't remember all their names.

13. *Never* had a moving violation ticket, only one parking ticket.

14. Graduated almost last from high school. Graduated with honors from Oswego State.

15. Been divorced.

16. Had grandson arrested for stealing coins. He went to jail for third time. If not in Al Anon, would not have done this.

17. So far survived prostate cancer.

18. Built my own house, where I still live, without mortgage.

19. While at convention of Al-Anon International in Pittsburgh, was trapped by a fire on twenty-third floor of high-rise hotel. Called daughter, she accused me of "always getting into trouble." Was finally cleared to use one stairway to descend. A little old lady wanted to go ahead of me in case I fell. Not a good idea. I weighed over two hundred pounds.

20. While at sea, taking picture of a jet plane, was blown off my feet and landed in steel fence on the deck edge. Again was at the wrong place at the wrong time!

21. While at sea, went through three typhoons—one in Yellow Sea and two in the Sea of Japan.

22. Participated in the Inchon invasion of South Korea on September 15, 1950.

23. Hold "Navy Unit Citation" plus six battle stars on Korean medal.

24. Taught school in Tupper Lake, grades 7–12, for twenty-six years.

25. Was an Eagle Scout.

26. Went to China in year 2000. Contracted food poisoning while in Beijing. Rushed to hospital and stayed there for

five days. While there, had no food and only foreign medication. After five days of watching China Olympics, started rooting for Chinese. Time to go home!

27. Am a Ham operator; call sign WA2GIU.

28. Our ship was shelled from shore batteries once or twice. They missed us. Were again in wrong place at wrong time.

29. Pilots were required to qualify for landing aboard aircraft carriers. Ensign Guffner (from Buffalo, NY) was killed. Another plane landed on his cockpit and cut him to pieces. Enlisted were asked to pick up some pieces on the deck. I picked up his helmet, but it contained the upper half of his head. Was not too hungry after this.

30. Now making rustic furniture and tying fishing flies.

31. Got lost in Paris; could not find my hotel. No one would speak English to me. It was getting dark, found a VISA store. One lady spoke English and she wrote out in French where to go. Gave this to taxi driver. Found hotel. Two years of high school French worthless.

32. While working at the Mallow Castle in Ireland, far away in Russia Chernobyl blew up. An atomic cloud floated over the British Isles and Ireland. Was warned by authorities . . . "Don't go outside for three days, don't eat any vegetables grown above ground, and don't drink any cow's milk." Now know why Irish drink booze.

33. Had quadruple bypass surgery in Albany hospital. Had verbal battle with head nurse. Upon leaving, she mooned me, "Don't come back, ever." I didn't like the food anyway.

34. While at cousin's wedding in San Francisco, had a verbal battle with priest before party. He was so mad he wanted to excommunicate me. Ho-hum.

35. Went to San Antonio for a reunion. The Menger Hotel was across the street from the Alamo (best hotel in San Antonio). Told the registrar I would like to pay in cash. Upon leaving she told me, "We don't accept cash." I disagreed. She called manager and threatened to call police. Just then my cousin from Sequin, Texas, appeared, and we

left for her house for a few days. Returned to hotel and gave them my VISA card for copying. Coward?

36. While ice fishing on Lake Simond on glare ice, lost creeper on right foot. Went after creeper, lost balance, and hit the ice hard. Broke right wrist. Had to learn how to wipe ass with left hand. Still do same now!

37. Was standing on a short ladder working on my truck. The ladder broke, and I fell and broke right kneecap. Next day was granddaughter's wedding. They forced me to dance with the bride. Ouch!

38. On a beautiful September day a few years ago, my daughter called to tell me that there was a fire on one of the islands in Big Tupper Lake. The fire department was looking for boats to transport firemen to the scene of the fire. Went down to the dock to unhook the boat. Unhooked tie down, stepped toward boat, and fell hitting metal tie downs hard. Went under water, water cold. Pain not too bad. Tried to walk. Got stuck in mud. Worked my way to walkway. Pain bad now. Got to house. Called son. Emergency room X-rayed broken shoulder, five broken ribs, one cracked. Three days in hospital. Lesson learned: cell phones don't work under water!

39. Tales from the South China Sea:
   a. Pilot and plane hit calm water and skipped like a stone. Pilot jumped on the wing. Helicopter right there, picked him up. Lucky guy. No wet feet.
   b. Pilot splashed in moderate rough water. He was picked up by helicopter soaking wet. First thing he did, run up to radio room and dip watch in 140-proof alcohol. Pilot saved. Watch working.
   c. On first offensive flight, Ensign Brogan flew off the bow and hit water. Fire broke out. I was working on deck edge, bringing out fifty-caliber ammo for next strike. Flames were coming at me. Hid out of heat. Pilot was burned but flew again after week recovery. Final thought . . . first day of action, what next?

d. Every third day was time to re-arm and take on gas and food stuffs. Many of us were on working parties. Had a hidden group to steal fruit juices and fruit cocktail. Would ferment juices in air duct (to avoid inspection) and drink when ready. Shades of Mr. Roberts!

e. While on work party, saw sailor lose his leg in bite of line. Medics were on him. He wanted to get up. Took him to sick bay. A black medic came up with a waste basket and picked up leg. The guy turned almost white.

f. Solving Problems:. How to get booze onto the ship when docked:

  1. Roll small bottles in kerchief (limit two). *Don't* put bottle in socks. Marines sometimes use night stick on socks = glass + blood. Officer started golfing; booze in bottom of golf bag. Marines don't check officers, just salute.

  2. Have hiding place. Big ships have many.

  3. Tell chief you are working for someone like an officer; they don't check them.

  4. Tell them you worked all night. Must sleep days.

  5. Have at least three liberty cards of different colors. Two usually have liberty in port.

  6. Tell chief you are a mess cook (like KP) and work nights only.

  7. One member had a wife working in a cannery on West Coast. She put booze in a no. 10 can and put on a fruit label. It passed through mail. Party time!

40. Tales at Sea

  a. Winter of 1951, snow on deck. A destroyer pulled up to re-arm or bring on provisions. Sailors on deck started throwing snowballs at destroyer. Smaller ship could not retaliate. Its skipper got hit in the head. A really mad message went to carrier's skipper to stop it and put on report anyone involved. Some people don't know what fun is! Must be from the South?

b.   We slept on 02 deck just above the hanger deck. There was a large bang. An ordinance man had plugged in a five-inch rocket on an airplane and it went off on the flight deck. The sailor was burned badly but recovered. At the time, a destroyer was crossing our ship's bow. The rocket just missed the smaller ship. Skipper radioed to our large ship, "You missed us, but for a second shot change heading fifteen degrees right."

c.   My bunk was in the forecastle (ship bow) with bunks three to four high. In bad weather, we were getting shaken out of bunks and banging about. Solution: tie ropes on two side openings, climb in end. Say a prayer we don't sink!

d.   The great ship anchored out about a half mile from shore. Motor whale boats were used as water taxis in rough weather. Four hazards: climb down ladder in rough seas; ride back, some seasick others drunk; most puking, wind baptized rear of boat; a feat of strength to climb that moving ladder up to carrier. One died, crushed between ship and boat.

e.   Placed on compartment detail. Plane landing above us. Propeller hit deck, went through eight-inch teak wood and one-inch steel. Hit bunks (three high), cut them to ribbons. First-class PO made us fix bunk. Lucky it happened when nobody was sleeping. Question: How come there is a hole over my bunk? Don't know nothing!

f.   Food and Water:

  i.   Our large ship had evaporators to produce fresh water. If one broke down, we had water hours. All fresh water was only at certain times. Coca-Cola machine would soon run out.

  ii.   Showers were done as follows: rinse and wash with salt water for two minutes. Rinse with fresh water for thirty seconds. Shore patrol or master at arms with clubs to do as above.

iii. Toilets (heads) were for six to eight people and open. Saltwater ran from high side to low side. Persons on high side would light large wads of toilet paper on fire and let them float down the stream of water. Term called getting "hot seated."

iv. Food was sometimes good, sometimes bad. Chicken, often served on Sunday, was called "Seagull." No fresh milk. After thirty to forty days at sea things went downhill. Still won't eat beans, green scrambled eggs, or SOS (shit on a shingle). SOS was hamburger or chipped beef in gravy on a slice of bread. Proof: when I went into the service, I weighed 175 pounds; when I came home, I was 149 pounds. Many of us would buy canned food and bring it on board. Sometimes c-rations tasted better.

41. Watches: On board ship, we were required to go on watch on the flight deck after operations ceased. Four hour watches went around the clock eight to twelve, twelve to four, four to eight, etc. The twelve-to-four watch at night was the worst. In rough weather, I have seen winds in excess of 75 mph. We put twenty-three steel cables on all planes so they wouldn't blow away. Other steel cables ran down the deck. We were anchored to them so *we* would not blow away. One time went to San Diego Airfield and was put on twelve-to-four watch. Went by jeep to the edge of the airfield, close to the Mexican border. Was handed a thirty-caliber carbine with ammo. Fired one only once in boot camp. Orders were to tell wetbacks (term for Mexicans) to stop, if not stopping, shoot. Question: "What is stop or halt in Mexican?" Answer: "Don't know."

42. Doors and Hatches: Under normal conditions, a person could walk from one place to another below the hanger bay. When General Quarters was sounded, all hatches were dogged (closed) with six or eight dogs (clamps). This sealed

each compartment and made it waterproof. "Where have you been?"

"Trapped below."

Okay.

43. Each deck had a stairway from one level to another with a heavy steel rail running the length of the stairs on each side. In emergencies, like General Quarters, the fastest way down was to slide down the rail. Injuries started mounting at sick bay from crashes. "All personnel are forbidden to slide down stairways!" Crew's reaction: Keep doing it; just don't get caught.

44. When aboard the USS *Valley Forge*, on payday counted over twenty poker games in progress. The big game was on 02 level (over the hangar deck). It was run by a chief petty officer. You had to have $1,000 to be admitted. A sailor was posted outside the poker room with his hand on a light switch to turn off power and hide evidence. I had to stick to penny-ante games. That is why our ship was known as the "Happy Valley." A great ship.

45. Crossed the International Date Line three times. Awarded the "Golden Dragon Certificate."

CHAPTER 3

Military Service: US Navy

1. From Syracuse, NY, I entered service on March 15, 1949. I was twenty years old.
2. I was sent to boot camp at the Great Lakes Naval Training Center in Illinois.
3. Then I went to school at the Naval Air Technical Training Center (NATTC), Memphis, Tennessee, where I went through four weeks of airman school and then eight months of electronics school. When I took a bus to town for the first time, I sat in the back of the bus. An old black lady came up to me and told me, "White folks have to sit in the front of the bus." I protested mildly but moved. Segregation was still the order of the day! This was seven or eight years before Rosa Parks protested. Her statue is in Washington, DC, and mine is not. Yet I was first?
4. The NATTC summer heat was mostly about 100°F with no air-conditioning. We lived in barracks with eight hours of school each day in Quonset huts. I graduated and then moved on.
5. I was transferred to Naval Air Station (NAS) Norfolk for four weeks of school to study advanced communication equipment, then to Naval Air Auxiliary Station (NAAS) Oceana, Virginia, just five miles from Virginia Beach.

Then I went into Air Group #6 (CVG #6) and fighter squadron VF-64, Free Lancers.

The Korean War broke out on June 15, 1950. That day the base was locked down and all hands started belting fifty-caliber ammo. Why? CVG #2 and CVG #6 were split. The readiest squadrons were put into CVG #2. So VF-64 (us) were now in CVG #2.

6. In August 1950, all enlisted personnel were put in a slow troop train and headed west. Our planes were flown to NAS San Diego. It took about seven or eight days of slow travel. We played poker and drank beer . . . like a vacation with pay!

7. In San Diego, we were sent directly to the USS *Boxer*. I should note that on the East Coast I was on the USS *Midway*. So I was somewhat familiar with the operations. They are very large ships and one can get lost on board. We left San Diego on August 24 for Hawaii. When we arrived, we went right into Pearl Harbor past the sunken USS *Arizona*.

8. Pilots did a little flying, and we also picked up four or five hundred Marines. They slept on cots on the hanger deck. At Sasebo, Japan, the Marines were dropped off and we went to sea after a couple days in Japan.

9. I was placed in a fifty-caliber belting crew working twelve hours on, twelve hours off as we crossed the Pacific. Our goal was to belt one million rounds of ammo before we saw action. Ironically, the one million rounds were shot off in less than six weeks of operation.

10. We joined Task Force #77, which was comprised of two or three carriers, a battleship or cruiser plus eight to sixteen destroyers. About one-half of the task force would leave to shell shore targets, returning after dark.

11. Our first action was the Inchon invasion on September 15, 1950. I was still working with the ammo detail and saw many small ships (LCTs, LCDs, and LSTs) heading toward Wilmido Island, South Korea. When on flight opera-

tions, my main job was to certify the functioning of the aircraft radios. This entailed moving between the planes while watching out for the rotating propellers and the prop wash. While working on deck once, I saw a plane crash and burn. Ens. Brogan, the pilot, was swimming on the outside edge of the flames. Brogan was burned on the skin that was exposed, but he was flying again in a week. What a start to war, avoid flames ammo safe.

12. Our task force operated in the Yellow Sea and the Sea of Japan. Our carrier had engine trouble, so we went back to the States in November. The troops have moved up into N. Korea. Some men went home for Christmas. The Chinese entered the war and CVG #2 was sent back on the Valley Forge after only twenty-one days in the States. The best meal I ever had aboard ship was the Christmas Day feast. It is now bitter cold and the flight deck had to be shoveled to get the planes off. Since I was from the North, I was placed on deck to work. As an example of the scope of operations, in three months we spent more ammo than any carrier in WWII.

13. We switched air groups from the Valley Forge to the Philippine Sea. The sea was very rough with high winds and angry waves. That day I witnessed twenty-two crashes. No pilots were lost, but it was a maintenance nightmare for the crews. The admiral that called for the switch made a mistake. We stayed on line until June and then headed home again.

14. In California, our new base was NAAB Santa Rosa, north of San Francisco. All new pilots mean training. West to Fallon, Nevada, for gunnery. Touch and go with LSO landing officer, sea qualification. Pilots had to have sharp skills to live. They are the best. One time while working with the LSO, I saw and heard a plane's engine sputtering. The pilot called "Mayday" and asked to land immediately. The tower operator put him into a landing pattern. The engine quit and his plane fell out of the air, crashed, and he died.

15. Before we went on our third cruise, I was transferred to Air Group 19 in Alameda, California. My squadron was VA-195. This squadron had AD Skyraiders. They were easier to work on than the F4U Corsairs. Air Group 19 was almost ready to go to sea aboard the Princeton. This time, I worked the flight deck for nine months repairing and maintaining the critical communications equipment on the aircraft. Life on deck was mostly routine, sprinkled with moments of fear. Fright was caused by such things as planes crashing and hitting where we were working, hung rockets or bombs flying down the deck from landing planes, etc. General Quarters (ship is locked down). All guns ready to fire. While in CVG #2, we were fired at from shore batteries once but they missed.

16. Back to the USA for the third time. The air group was sent to Moffett Field south of San Francisco. This base had huge lighter-than-air hangars with their own atmosphere inside. A fine rain inside yet sunny outside?

17. After three years, nine months, and nine days of service, I was sent to Treasure Island for discharge.

18. It should be noted that air group #2 was the most decorated air group of the Korean War. Air group #2 lost thirty-one men, mostly killed in action. Also had three POWs. Air Group #19 lost fourteen men mostly KIA.

19. I hold the following decorations: Korean Medal with six battle stars, UN Medal, Occupation Medal, Good Conduct Medal, China Service Medal, two Korean Medals, plus the Navy Unit Citation. I saw three people get killed in operations; they are the true heroes.

"One death is one too many."

CHAPTER 4

Tupper Lake

After finishing military service, I attended college at Oswego State University with the aid of the GI Bill. When I graduated with a degree in education, I moved with my wife to the Adirondack Mountains in the central northern part of New York State. The Adirondack Park contains almost six million acres and is the largest state park in our nation. (In fact, it is larger than any *national* park in the lower forty-eight states.) It is comprised of 45 percent state-owned land and 55 percent private property. The territory inside the Park has about three thousand lakes, twelve major rivers, and hundreds of smaller streams. The entire region is larger than the state of Vermont. For example, Hamilton County, one of the counties in the park, is so rural there are no stoplights on any of its intersecting roads.

In 1945, I visited Tupper Lake, NY, with the Boy Scouts where we stayed at Little Wolf Pond. Going into town one night, the fire whistle sounded at nine o'clock. All teenagers had to be off the streets. Would this work today? I went fishing at Underwood Bridge at the outlet of Raquette Pond and latched into a large northern pike. I fought the pike for fifteen minutes and then the line broke.

I found a job in Tupper Lake teaching shop at the junior high and high school levels. The shop was a mess, and it took many hours of hard work to bring it up to standards. I learned that the former teacher allowed the students to have races on the floor with vibrat-

21

ing sanders. He often sent students out to get food and drinks. So I introduced the students to military discipline with guidelines of expected conduct. The students started to learn then, I think.

One day, a kid was yelling, "Power to the people." I wondered if he was a communist in the class. When I asked him, he said, "Would you turn on the power so we could use the machine?" He was a good American.

I shot my first northern New York buck as a guest of the Big Simond Hunting Club. Now I've been a member for fifty-four years. This club was called the "Teachers Club" as many local teachers and Albany area educators were members. It was a chance to let your hair down, drink a few beers, play poker or cribbage, and relax without student interference. A few of the unique members were Martin P., Ozzie and Jack (known as "Pear Shape"). Martin was a graduate of Julliard in New York City. He was employed as a fish biologist in our local DES. His liking for the bottle is undeniable. Coming home one night at twenty below, he lost his door key. So he tried to crawl in through the doggie door and got stuck halfway in. One-half of his body was freezing. The other half was hot with the dog licking his face. He got free after quite a struggle.

Another time, Martin went camping at an old log lean-to. Trying to go to sleep he heard a gnawing sound. He discovered a porcupine under the lean-to eating the floor boards. Grabbing his muzzle-loading pistol, he crawled under the lean-to and tried to solve the problem. The pistol blast not only killed the beast but also ignited the nitrate-rich scat that had built up over the years. The blast hit him in the face, and he swore that "he was picking out shit" from his mouth for two or three days.

Martin lived at his disheveled camp, which he called "Dismal Seepage." The place was heated with a woodstove and his couch was packed with carrion beetles. Martin was a good friend and is missed.

The father-and-son hunting team of Ozzie and Jack ("Pear Shape") were putting on a deer drive on one of Lake Simond's small mountains. Ozzie to son (Pear Shape), "You drive (walk) up the mountain."

Pear Shape responded, "Not again."

Ozzie said, "Get going now."

Pear Shape's responded, "I'll take the gun, but no shells."

Ozzie said, "Get going."

Pear Shape answered, "F___ you, Dad."

Tupper Lake is a small village of about five thousand residents. The people are very friendly, a blue-collar group, with emphasis on logging and tourism. Sunmount Hospital is the main source of employment. The people like to give each other nicknames. Anyone living in town for a number of years can fill in their actual last name.

Some of the nicknames are Peako, Vulture, Cabbage and his son Brussel Sprouts, Pinhead, Woody, Chip, Kick, Buck, Moose, Rat (Muskrat), Weasel, Fishhook, Pig Ears, Cigar, Pee Wee, Bear, Bozo, Zulu, Canoe, Slim, Pear Shape, Boogy, Beaver, 3 Fingers, Sack, Bad Back, Cats, Animal, Butch, DoDo, Chuckles, Barrel, Chemical, Pisser, Nutsy, Tinker Bell, Dweller, Buddy, Krit, Ducky, Tuffy, Norm, Thumper, Ho Train, Zombie, Popcorn, Skip, Beard', etc. If you know someone from Tupper Lake, an older person, have them try to identify the holders of these nicknames. Ninety percent correct is excellent!

Each of the four seasons has something to offer the residents of the Adirondacks. Spring is called the mud season. As the earth defrosts, it contains a lot of water, which makes mud. Things bloom, a welcome sight, but it is also the start of the bug season—black flies, mosquitos, no-see-ums, biting flies, and hornets and bees. Bugs are not active if the temperature drops into the low forties.

Summer is great for outdoor sports, fishing and boating on the many ponds and lakes. There are many public campsites to enjoy. It never gets too hot, and summer seldom lasts too long. Cool nights are common.

The fall leaves are outstanding up to about October 1. The colors are visited by many folks who are called "Leaf Peepers." But it is a short season.

Winter can be a problem. The coldest I have seen is forty-two degrees below zero. Winter can bring snow from November until May. A big problem can be power outages in bitter cold weather. Solution: have a generator, burn wood, use propane heaters and electric heaters (with a generator). The air quality is great. If you have breathing problems, our air is pure. Pollen levels in the fall are low, especially allergens like Golden Rod, etc.

Ice fishing has many followers. Hunting lasts for six or seven weeks, a sportsman's paradise. I love living in Tupper Lake!

CHAPTER 5

More Snippets from the Past

1. While having a brief stop at Hawaii, I went to the Royal Hawaiian Hotel at Waikiki Beach. Found a revolving bar and had a few drinks. Fell off the bar. Couldn't find seat and needed help to get back on bar. Evils of drink a factor!

2. I was in Ireland to work for Mallow Castle. In Ireland, St. Patrick's Day is a holy day. When I started for church, I ran into a tinker boy selling shamrocks. I told the boy I only had American money. It was okay, so I gave him fifty cents for some shamrocks. He ran away without giving me my purchase. So I went on to church, and there I saw the same boy outside the church. "You ripped me off, boy."

    "That was not me, that was me brother." Conclusion: All tinkers are thieves, but smart thieves.

3. Sleeping in the bow of a large carrier. Let's try something! Found steel marbles and placed them on the steel deck. As ship rolled, marbles would roll across deck and hit steel bulkhead (wall) with a loud BANG, then bounce about. Fun to watch. The phone rings, "This is commander so-and-so. Stop that noise now or else." He is no fun. Tales from Mr. Roberts.

4. Tried to make skis from two barrel staves and tried them out on a steep hill. Could not stand, too much camber. "Let's

slide with American Flyer," two rail snow sled. Sharpened runners until all rust gone and they shine. Go to hill where three boys (brothers) live. One boy at bottom of hill. If a car comes, we must stop run by turning sled on its side. If no car, slide through intersection for about three hundred more feet. Fun, but dangerous. We don't care.

5. The father of three boys on the hill caught them smoking cigarettes. Father brought out four cigars. "This will make a man out of you." All four smoked. Father got sick.

6. How to save gas, my father's method:
   a. Don't drive, walk.
   b. Don't brake a moving car . . . let it glide to a stop or turn.
   c. On steep hill, take car out of gear, turn off engine, and glide to a stop. No automatic cars those days!
   d. Catch people stealing gas. He caught the thief and tackled him. Thief pleaded or his life. He let him go never to be seen again. No police . . . neighborhood justice.

7. On a revisit to South Korea on the 50th anniversary of the Inchon landing people came up and in broken English said, "Thank you for saving our country." Makes you feel good.

8. While in Japan, I hailed a taxi to travel back to ship. Taxi had a wood-fired propulsion system and steam convertor. About every fifth stop for a traffic light, the driver would run back to the rear of the taxi and throw more wood into the boiler. It ran just fine. To hell with pollution and rainforests!

9. The chief petty officer, with over twenty years of service, stopped a young sailor. The sailor was disheveled, hat on crooked, uniform a mess, and he saluted with his l e f t hand (a no-no).
   Chief asked, "How long you been in the navy, boy?"
   Sailor answered, "All day, sir."

10. Martin P., of Big Simond Club fame, philosophized after missing an attempt to make it to the outdoor toilet facilities (outhouse), "Tis a dirty bird that fouls his own nest."

11. Many years ago, the French Village (in Tupper Lake) was a small settlement near the log mill. One Russian worker saw his woodpile slowly disappear. He decided to catch the thief. He drilled out a chunk of hardwood, filled it with black powder, plugged the hole, and put it in his woodpile. A few nights later, there was a loud explosion and fire in one of the nearby cabins. Another example of street justice!

12. Old time hunting method: two hunters, one ferret, and one dog. Put ferret into rabbit hole, out comes the rabbit. Send dog after rabbit. Rabbit makes a circle heading for his hole. Shoot rabbit. Get ferret out of hole by dropping in a string with a carrot on the end. A ferret is like a weasel and follows food up. Grab him. If not coming out of hole, must dig him out. Yes, it was legal in those days.

13. Dirty song for kids: "Dirty Lil, Dirty Lil, lives on top of the garbage hill. Never washes, never will, (Note: with tongue make a vibrating sound) Dirty Lil."

    "Dirty Hank, Dirty Hank, lives inside a septic tank. Never washes, never will. He got married to Dirty Lil."

14. In the twenties, thirties, and forties, boys played marbles for recreation and profit. Local roles may differ. This is what we did. Draw a circle in the soft earth about one and one half to two feet in diameter. Each player, usually two to four, puts five to eight marbles in the circle. Then they draw straws (grass) to see who shoots first. With great skill try to knock one or more of the marbles outside the circle with your shooting marble, "shooter." Make sure your shooter exits circle. If it doesn't, it stays in the circle. You keep the marbles, you knock out. Pass shooting position to next in line in order of straw length. Rules: No hunching (finger or shooter over the circle line). Arguments were settled by flipping a coin. Not all kids those days had coins. Some of the riffraff had great skills. I lost most times.

15. A naval sick trick. Don't feel like working today. Take some yellow lye soap and put it under both armpits. If fever starts go to sick bay. Corpsman, "I see you have a fever. Take

some APCs and take two days off. Here is a chit for you to show superiors so you don't get in trouble."

"Thanks." I never tried this, but they say it works?

16. Song from North Cork Radio, Ireland. "The Devil is dead. This Devil is dead and living in Killarney. The Devil is dead, he joined the British army." An IRA song.

17. Being a mess cook is just like slavery. Up at 5:00 AM, eat breakfast; 6:00 AM start with regular chow. Work in the scullery cleaning dirty dishes. Regular mess starts between 7:00–8:00 AM and lasts for three hours. Feed two thousand men. Our work lasted up until midday lunch and lasted until 3:00 PM. One hour off. Start again at 4:00 PM for night meal. Work until about seven to eight o'clock. We slept in hammocks tied between two steel posts. Clothes were tied to one end of bunk.

One night, some guy reached into my back pocket and stole my wallet. I chased him up two or three decks in bare feet but lost the thief. Luckily, he just took money but left all my identification. Lucky day. It's a problem to replace all lost items. He did not get much money. Every morning, we had to take the hammocks down and store them out of the way. The PA system would announce, "Heave to and trice up." In Navy terms, this means "Get up now and put bunk away."

18. An anchor pool is a wager for the exact time the ship's anchor is dropped. The bet may vary from $100 to $1,000. $100 × 60 minutes equals a total pot of $6,000. The pot would be divided into the "Big Pot" of $4,600 for the exact time, two smaller pots of $400 each for one minute before or after the exact time and $600 for the man running the pool. It is illegal to gamble aboard ship. I won $25 from the side of a smaller pool.

19. *Making Adirondack Guide Boats*: This boat type originated in Northern New York. Years before motorized traffic, it did all the heavy work and still is the best trout fishing boat. I was lucky to take a course in making guide boats

through the North Country Community College. This was an accredited course with instructor Carl Hathaway, an expert builder. The course was two semesters long. My son, Tom, was a working lumberjack, so I could get spruce roots for ribs plus deck coverings and planking made from pine or cedar. Anywhere from four hundred to five hundred hours are needed to complete a guide boat. These boats are light weight, twenty-five to fifty pounds, so they are very portable. I am the only human to make a guide boat in Europe (Ireland). It was enjoyable work. No, I don't want a statue of me in the town center.

CHAPTER 6

North Woods Living and
a Little Philosophy

1. Wood fires are still found in the North Country. Some are used for emergency situations (like no electric power), other people use wood to heat their houses to save on the high cost of fuel oil. Wood prices may be in excess of $50 per face cord (8'×4'×12"). Many people cut, haul, and split their own wood. They say it heats you twice. Hardwoods like beech, birch, maple, ash, and cherry are the most used. Softwoods burn fast and produce pitch. The smell of a wood fire is the smell of earlier peoples surviving the cold, northern winters. Someone asked, "In your area, what are your raw materials"? Answer: beech, birch, and babies.

2. Many think that fishing is more exciting than hunting. Fishing gives us more action more often. Hunting takes time in the woods, use of expensive weapons and clothing, shooting skills plus patience. Children like to catch fish. For them, size is not the problem. Who knows, if our government falls apart (no power, no fuel, no phone or internet) survival will depend on our basic outdoor and survival skills.

After a deer is down, the work begins. With a sharp knife carefully open the cavity, remove the liver and heart. Cut out stomach, gall bladder without puncturing to prevent getting any foul-smelling stuff into the opening. With a small knife cut around the deer's anus to free intestines. Don't let poop enter deer cavity. I slosh inside of animal with water mixed with baking soda. The old hunters drag deer out of the woods and hang the deer for about a week if outside temperature is 40°F or colder. Next skin the animal from neck to lower legs. Cut out inner and outer loins called back straps. Cut off shoulders—they make a great roast if fixed with a few bacon strips to add grease and flavor. Cut out rear leg muscles removing outside skin-like covering (covering contains gamey taste). Cut meat into one-fourth-inch strips for steak. Less choice meat is used for hamburger. I mix in bacon to add grease and flavor to the meat. Sausage is also made from hamburger plus spices. Cook steak with a greased hot iron frying pan. Put meat in and flip it over. Don't overcook! Venison is hard to beat for flavor.

3. Bears live around my backwoods Adirondack home. Do I like bears? Yes. Have I shot bears? Yes. When bears cross human boundaries, which is seldom, I must act! For example, after midnight a large bear broke a window in my shed door, pushed the rear wall out, and pushed out any garbage as well as an eighty-pound bag of cement. Garbage was spread out all over my land. Solutions: call the DEC, shoot the animal, or keep garbage out of the shed? I picked the latter. Bears are more active before or coming out of hibernation. Mothers are protective of cubs.

Once, perhaps thirty-five years ago, my neighbor's wife yells, "The school bus just went up the road to turn around and a bear is on my front lawn. The two girls can't get out of the house." Grabbing my gun, I jumped in my car, stopping close to the bear. The school bus then pulls up and opens its door. I yelled a mighty noise and the bear ran off. All is now safe for the girls to enter the bus. Let's consider this: If I shot the bear, all the kids would say, "Mommy, a big, bad man with a gun shot a baby bear!" Another close call?

4. Our Adirondack Mountains are just over five thousand feet in elevation. The winters are colder than outer surrounding areas. Forty below is not uncommon. Ice covers our lakes and ponds to the depth of two to three feet of blue ice. (Blue ice is solid ice.) It is hard to convince people living here that global warming exists. Yet Mother Nature may cause global warming? But we humans cannot change this. Perhaps we should ban all motor vehicles or reduce the world population by 95 percent? These radical solutions won't work.

    Will this global warming help with my fuel bills? No, because the price of oil and gas still shoots up. People ask me, "Why do you live in the woods? And in cold weather, what do you do?" My false answer, "Oh, I check the mail and watch TV." I'm really always busy tying flies, building rustic furniture, getting into trouble like breaking bones, etc. Here the air is pure and we are free of big city congestion and high crime. Remember, this is the only place where I can pee off my front porch and not get arrested.

5. My favorite type of music is country and folk music. In my early youth, I would walk from high school to my home, about three miles. Stopping at my great-aunt's house was a welcome break as they always had one or two cookies. They had a wind-up Victrola, which let me hear the Carter Family (first country singers). On my home, crystal set on clear nights I could pick up Del Rio, Texas, a country radio station. This station used unlimited power because their antenna was located in Vasconia, Mexico. The USA had transmission limits, but not in Mexico.

    When stationed in Memphis, Tennessee, I saw, on stage, Ernie Ford and Burl Ives. Yes, this redneck Yankee was hooked.

6. Battle of the Varmints: As weather cools mice invade my castle. They like to eat peanut butter–laced traps. These deer mice are smart. How can they eat off the peanut butter and not get caught? I don't know! They *are* smart! One mole lived with me for two years. They are fast and shy of traps. A red squirrel is a different, big problem. Last week, I saw one climb down a tree headfirst. Wow? In my home, I started to find furnishings on a higher level pushed off shelves. Pictures, candlesticks, and other memorabilia on the floor. Was this an earthquake, a gravity switch, or just a hungry red varmint? He was too smart to get into a trap. I finally cornered him in my laundry room by closing a door. When I opened an outside door, he vanished. Hope he learned a lesson . . . don't mess with Wild Bill.

7. Some birds live with us all year. Others, like warblers, are just passing through. The ducks, geese, and loons summer here and then move on as water supplies freeze up. The winter birds, like ruffed grouse, pesky ravens (they have chased out the crows), chickadees, nut hatches, gold finches, and a few woodpeckers stay all year. I do hunt grouse for food, but populations vary. Excuse me for not mentioning all species as it might take pages. I like the birds with colorful feathers.

8. Exercise and physical training is the second battle of the bulge. After some accidents and operations, I was placed in our local PT unit. The pain endured is well worth the time in seeking recovery. A person doing manual labor has no need for physical training. Lack of exercise and a poor diet causes weight gain. Taking fat off your body is a never-ending battle. Some win and others lose. Some eat to live; others live to eat. Who wins if our weight goes up or down? The clothing industry wants belly change, which translates into profits.

9. Children and grandchildren are great to have contact with, but it's not good to live with them. I have about twelve grandchildren and five great-grandchildren. When they all

get together, I now have trouble remembering their names. They call it "old timer's disease." At least twice a year, I have a family cookout, on July 4 and Labor Day. This event promotes family unity. We have games like horseshoes, tug-o-war, swing (rite of passage), and children's spitting contest. After such events, I crave peace and quiet. Can you blame me? Now you know why I'm somewhat unstable at times.

10. The wooden Adirondack guide boat was the only means of transportation over our waterways. In the early years of population increase, it was light enough to carry from one lake to another (called portage) in the back country where roads don't exist. It was used for hunting, fishing, plus transportation of people and building materials.

This type of wood boat is only made by skilled craftsmen in the Adirondack region. The only exception was a wood guide boat built under my tutelage by Harry Miltner(?) in E. Wenatchee, Oregon.

Up to 40 to 50 spruce ribs are cut from the natural curvature of tree roots and finished by hand. The curved grain spruce is then dried for several years. Spruce, a soft wood, is stronger than some hard woods. The ribs are fastened with brass wood screws to a shaped bottom board made from knot-free pine or cedar. The bow and stern stems are made from spruce and fastened to the bottom board. The boat is then flipped upside down. The outside is made from quarter cut pine or cedar planks, five-eighth-inch or less thick. The planking is then shaped with beveled edges and cut to fit the boat's shape. Depending on the length of the guide boat about four thousand to five thousand copper tacks and brass screws are used. The gunwales are made from cherry. Then the decks are added, seats are caned, oars are carved, and finish applied. All together four hundred to five hundred man-hours are required for each guide boat. The finished guide boat is a thing of beauty and quite seaworthy. Joe Spadaro, a builder in a nearby village, stated, "You don't have to be crazy to build a guide boat, but it helps."

11. Gambling. Like it or not, life is a gamble. Some win, some lose. I enjoy casino gambling, but I seldom win. My favorite gambling game is slot machine poker. I guess it is okay as long as I don't lose more than I can afford or become addicted to the games. Remember, it also helps the Native Americans, a real charity?

12. Some jobs I have done over the years: Shoveled snow for neighbors, was a "soda-jerk" in the family store, raised pigeons, grew a family vegetable garden, electronic technician, fourth loader on 40mm guns, mess cook in scullery (this was as close to slavery as one can get, twelve to sixteen hours per day), teacher grades 7–12, house builder, maker of rustic furniture, tied flies, made feather earrings, builder of boats, etc. For fourteen years, I was the sole caregiver of elderly parents (mother lived to age ninety-nine). I never quite retired, just changed jobs!

13. The climate is changing as it has over the past centuries. Where I live was once covered with tons of glacier ice. The evidence is all over my property, large boulders rounded by water or ice, some weighing many tons, and small, round ponds, some less than one hundred yards wide. It looks like chunks of ice fell from many miles up onto soft melted soil. Scientists now claim our earth's axis is slowly changing. Results unknown? Scientists and others are now getting on the "Green Bandwagon." Some people are earning big salaries lecturing about climate change. They would be more honest if they said, "This has been going on for millions of years and nothing can be done about it." Some time, the sun will stop, the sun's rays will turn deadly, earthquakes will explode, and objects from outer space may hit us as was done in the past. I don't think the earth will end on December 21, 2012, so let's not worry.

14. Understanding in a Higher Power, Belief in Supernatural Beings: Most ancient cultures believe in one or more gods. Yet some believe we came from apes. However, the teaching of the Holy Bible states that God made the earth in six

days, resting on the seventh day. However, many people say we just evolved?

One day, while watching a daddy longlegs spider, I noticed how it moved. Each leg joint, only one-thirty-second of an inch in size, moved in unison with its other legs controlled by the spider's brain. What a complex living being! If many scientists smarter than Einstein cannot produce a living, moving daddy longlegs spider, I doubt that he could have evolved by chance. I hate to break their bubble. When science creates a living spider, then I will believe in some of the evolutionary theories. Remember, a theory is just a suggested possibility of what might happen. Yes, climate changes, people differ, animals change, but all within nature's limitations. Remember, species only propagate within set rules. Birds don't mate with rabbits. A Higher Power does exist for our benefit.

Someone asked me what my favorite color was. I replied, "Green." They said, "Then you are one of us."

"No," I said, "I just like green as a color, nothing else. After all I'm 25 percent Irish."

PS: During muzzle loading deer season, on October 15, 2012, I downed a deer with open sights at over ninety-three paces at eighty-four years old! This is why they call me "Hawkeye."

CHAPTER 7

More North Country Nonsense

1. North Country Weather:

    How cold it gets depends on your elevation and how close you live to the North Pole. At the same time, consider these factors, the amount of forest cover, and your closeness to bodies of water. Lake water is like a hot water bottle; it holds heat and also cold. Living in the woods is always cooler than living in town.

    A person asked, "Why don't you cut more trees so you can see more of the lake?" Trees are like a snow fence; they block the wind. A lakeside wind may blow at 20 mph, but at my house, located 150 feet away from the lake, it is nil.

    Most people don't like below-zero weather. Our fear is loss of electric power, as a house can freeze in a matter of hours. My home has access to a portable generator, two wood fires as well as a kerosene heater. Some folks put antifreeze in hot water pipe, take care not to put it in drinking water pipes. Denatured alcohol is poisonous!

    While assisting in amateur radio repairs on top of Mt. Morris (elevation 3,552 ft.), the temperature was below zero with a steady wind of 40 mph. Even wearing very heavy clothing our bodies could only tolerate ten minutes of exposure. The cold felt like pin needles on your skin followed by numbness. Thank God we had a small heated radio shack to warm up.

Some lumberjacks lived down the road from me. While passing their cabin, I saw smoke coming from their pickup truck. I stopped to inquire if there was a problem? With a French accent, they stated, "No, we build a fire under the truck to heat the engine." Did they ever lose a truck? "Not yet, but we keep our insurance up to date."

In the past, using a kerosene lantern or a hundred-watt lightbulb and an old blanket over the hood did the job. When all measures fail, if possible call AAA.

2. How to Deal with Money:

Some wise man said, "Money is the root of all evil." Possibly true. In today's society, one problem is credit (hope to pay later). Other factors are credit cards, TV commercials, food ads, $19.95 deals, and other "free" deals. So they say, "The only thing free is the air you breathe."

The second problem is income vs. spending. Not a good example is our federal government. But how can we save with all these bills? Bills are from indiscriminate spending. Always buy newest fashion. Look what the neighbors have! Let's start with a budget. Write down what money goes where. For example, if groceries cost $40 per week, could it be cut to $30 without compromising nutrition? Use coupons. Also two-for-one sales, plus meat marked down because of age and older pastries. Many quick stops have weekend jobs. Many younger people do not understand saving. Put away any amount of money each week for one year. One dollar a week in one year equals $52. Put away $10 a week for one year equals $520. Do this consistently over a length of time. If this doesn't work for you, start putting pocket change away every time you shop.

An old German philosopher once stated, "Get a good education in a profession, but learn a trade skill as a backup if this fails." Your work possibility is now much improved. Good wisdom!

3. North Country Characters:
    A) Mitchell Sabatis was a Native American. He resided in the Long Lake, NY, area. He was a boat builder who is credited with making one of the first wood guide boats. Mitchell would disappear into the woods and return with small quantities of gold. He never revealed his secret.
    B) Old Rat Lavoie was from French Canadian heritage, living and working in Tupper Lake New York. During WWII a Canadian bomber crashed in Tupper Lake in a swampy section, on the east end of the Lake, a crew from Canada was sent to raise the craft. The Canadian crew could not raise the bomber. Rat Lavoie was contacted to do the job. Using logs, leverage he raised the motor (stuck in the mud), and other parts of the plane.
    C) Basketball teams in small towns are very competitive. Some older men were verbally abusing the visiting teams. Two adults were banned forever. "Cabbage" and "Kick" were irate, but kicked out. Rumor has it they voted no to all school budgets.
    D) Buying cheap blue jeans was a mistake. The pockets were ripping and keys and coins started falling out. Idea . . . let's super glue the pocket holes. Holding the fabric with fingers put on liberal amounts of super glue. Discovered fingers were sticking to the pockets. Ripped the fingers away only to find four fingers were stuck together. Should I call 911? No, I'm no wimp! With great effort, fingers were ripped apart. Great, no blood or lost skin. Lesson learned . . . super glue is super sticky.
    E) A Christmas Story: One day just before Christmas vacation, "Let's send the art department a Christmas gift. Let's send Bummer." Bummer liked the idea. The shop girls started decorating Bummer. Curled wood shavings plus color, bulbs made from wood plus color

and colored thread wrapped around his body. Given a corridor pass from shop to art, he was a hit with the art gang. Bummer liked the attention, but finally they threw him out. "No, Bummer, you're not wearing that home. Clean him up."

F) Hunting Tupper Style: A couple of local hunters shot a deer out of season. They placed the deer in the back seat of their car. Proudly driving down our main street, hiding their prize, the deer started kicking. Just stunned, it started making noises and our heroes panicked. The pair rushed out of town to a desolate area, and they euthanized the poor beast. "Why does the back seat of the car smell like a dead cat?"

"Just open the window."

G) After hunting season, a local family went camping on their island camp. The week got very cold, two degrees to five degrees below zero. Ice formed two to three inches thick on the lake. The people were isolated as the small camp wood boat could not break the thick ice. A neighbor called, "Could you rescue them?"

"No, but I will help."

I called my neighbor Bob, "Would you like to die today?"

"No, but I will help." Without weight in the bow the fifteen-foot aluminum could not break the ice. Put into boat life jackets, oars, and a ten-horse mercury outboard. Had to break about two miles of solid ice. Picked up victims and headed for the boat launch. Let passengers off, not even a "thank-you." Any hole in the boat would have been a disaster. No cell phones then. Yes, another close call.

H) Snow machines became popular in the sixties and the seventies. Norm and I went on a short run. We came upon a machine with engine running but stuck well into the alders. Since the snowmobiler had been drinking, we noticed a bird feather on his helmet. His name . . . "Ivan the Bird." We got the machine out, and he jumped on his skidoo and took off. Last we heard of him was word that he drove through the bar's door into the bar area and ordered a beer. A good reason to drink but don't drive.

I) "Barrel" was at the bar in the old Iroquois Hotel with his chums. After several drinks, a fisherman came in and tried to sell some worms. Barrel stated that for some money, he would eat some worms. Money started mounting on the bar, possible over $20. The money said he would not eat worms. Barrel took a quick drink and grabbed a couple of night crawlers followed by another drink. Now he was a bar hero! He picked up the money and left for home. The next night, "Bummer," hearing of Barrel's feat, started drinking with the boys. He said, "Give me a couple of worms," and down they went followed by a drink. The crew said, "We didn't bet any money." Bummer replied, "I forgot." Which one is the better bar hero?

by
William (Bill) Lawson Crouse

Credits
John Mahar
Crystal Pascarella Swenson
Theresa Lindsay
Linda Farnsworth
Victoria Pickering

THE NAVY WAY

The coordination of enlisted men and pilots in perfect harmony in combat off Korea, during the United Nations operation, to stem communist aggression was awesome.

On June 25, 1950 to July 27, 1953, the author William (Bill) Crouse AT-3 Air Group #2; his perspective at that time, aboard four aircraft carriers, the USS *Boxer*, USS *Valley Forge*, USS *Philippine Sea*, and USS *Princeton*.

This book is dedicated to Captain Dave Leue', a member of Air Group #2. Dave retired with many years' service in the United States Navy. Dave was an excellent pilot flying the F4U Corsair in the Korean War. He was one of my trusted friends and had a hard time to beat a record with over 328 combat missions in two wars. He has since passed away and will be thoroughly missed.

ABOUT THE AUTHOR

Born in Syracuse, NY, and attended local schools, graduated from Christian Brothers Academy (CBA) in 1946. Our family ran a small neighborhood grocery store. I worked in the store during most of the war years. I had an interest in model air planes. I joined the Navy just to seek a change, went to boot camp at Great Lake Illinois, then to electronics school in Memphis, Tennessee. I selected a fighter squadron VF#64 in Oceana, Virginia. I was discharged from Treasure Island in California in 1952.

I started to work in house construction, was married, using the GI Bill, I graduated from SUNY Oswego. I moved to Tupper Lake, NY, in the Adirondack Mountains and taught industrial arts, driver education, and mechanical drawing. After twenty-six years, I retired but resumed house and camp construction. I built seventeen Adirondack Guide Boats plus rustic furniture, tied flies, made fly earrings, was a caretaker, fishing guide, and movie projectionist.

Shortly after I was born, the Great Depression started. The entire world was affected. In the United States, banks closed, the value of money plunged, some stocks dropped to zero, and all investors lost something. Production in factories slowed, workers were terminated, and some people were placed on relief; food stuff were given so they could survive. Some, in desperation, committed suicide. In the 1930s, a huge dust storm engulfed the country. In Syracuse, NY, a west wind sent dust to the Eastern States. Our mother would cover the "house windows to prevent it from entering the cracks." The conditions had people moving; some abandoned their farms and headed to California. Men looking for jobs would hitch rides on railroad box cars. They were called "bums." At the same time, there were riots in large cities. Most cities had 20 to 30 percent unemployment, yet rural farms only had 10 to 15 percent unemployment, and they were lucky to have food and cattle. Even in cities, the populous with land started gardens. I raised chickens but roosters crowing at 5:00 AM put a halt to that. Some had "soup kitchens" to stave off hunger. "Help is coming!"

Federal money was flushed into the economy. The WPA (Work Progress Administration) was formed to build roads, bridges, sewer lines, and other infrastructures. Father had to quit the store to go to work for the WPA. He was out of work for one year. We were aided by grandfather and some odd jobs he could find. The CCC (Civilian Construction Corporation) was formed where state parks, planting of trees, and doing trail work was done. Father worked also at "Pine Camp," a military base that put in sewers; it is now called "Fort Drum."

World War II started with the bombing of Pearl Harbor by the Japanese. That put an end to the depression, but during the war, everything was scarce. All prices were frozen to stop inflation and everyone was required to have ration cards (even the babies). Clothing, shoes, meat, butter, canned goods, gasoline (eighteen cents per gallon) needed stamps or no sale. My Uncle Henry was drafted, so my father went back into the family grocery store. In my boyhood, I joined the Boy Scouts and built model airplanes, broke windows playing, had a bang site cannon," which shot birds with my BB gun, and smoked leaves in the cellar. Father set up a shooting gallery in the cellar, and as I was holding my loaded .22 rifle in the vertical position, my little five-year-old brother reached up and pulled the trigger. The .22 shot up through the living room floor and hit the dining room table, nearly missing my mother. You talk about an angry woman; she said, "You could have shot me!" Father said nothing when he came home.

We did everything for the war effort—collected paper (the price shot up $1 per hundred weight), had a victory garden, and canned food. Father had a gas card for only six gallons per week. I worked in the store as a "soda jerk" throughout my high school years. Strangers would come looking for beer and cigarettes—and this is when I learned to lie with a straight face; they were stored in the backroom for regular customers.

I was a poor high school student but graduated from high school with a minor in history, major in science. I started working in the store plus a cooperative grocery warehouse. The future looked dull, so I joined the Navy on March 15, 1949. I was sworn in at Albany, NY, took a train ride to my hometown of Syracuse, NY, and then onto Great Lakes, Illinois, for boot camp; will I ever see home again?

Our mentor was a Chief Petty Officer with gold insignia. His power over us was just shy of being a God Chief. He had over thirty years' service, and I assumed he was close to retirement. His first statement went like this: "*To do things, there is a right way, a wrong way, but henceforth, you will do things the Navy Way.*" We, as recruits, had to salute him as if he was an Officer. To show his authority while marching, we had to pivot on one heel. One recruit was wrong; the Chief stomped on his toe hard: "Now pivot on the sore foot."

A quick joke: Another Chief saw a new sailor in complete disarray. His uniform was dirty and not on correctly. His hat was on incorrectly and he saluted with his left hand (a no-no right away). The Chief asked, "How long have you been in the Navy, son?"

Responding, the recruit said, "All day, Sir."

Boot camp under Chief Tandy included naval, history, marching (with fake guns), swimming, gunnery first aid, and other necessary classes. We competed with other recruits for the Red Roster Flag. My class was listed as 09 (nine weeks) as 1950 was the year of graduation. I was granted seven days leave and had to report to NATTC, Memphis, Tennessee, to electronic school. Most of our nine months was spent studying basic electronics in aircraft. If you failed weekly tests, you were to repeat that week over again. Fail a second time and you were gone with no skills. This is how I learned to study correctly. We lived in old WWII Quonset Huts, no air-conditioning, four hours of theory followed by four hours of practice on radio gear. I went on the bus for a six-mile journey to Memphis, Tennessee, to look things over. I went to the back of the bus and an old black lady said, "White folks have to sit in the front of the bus." I protested but finally moved to the front. I did not realize that everything was segregated. Rosa Parks has her statute in Washington, DC, but I was first—no statute for me. My friend, Rodney Barber (a New Yorker), who failed into my class (09-50), he passed so he moved onto next week.

I went to NAS (Naval Air Station) in Norfolk, VA, for three weeks' training. I went to town and saw that famous sign: "Dogs and sailors keep off the grass!" Depending on your grade in school, you could pick the duty stations; some were overseas. Rodney and I picked Air Group #6 (CVG)—Carrier Air Group but both were in different squadrons.

Air Group #6 had one squadron of panther jets and three squadrons of corsairs followed by one squadron of sky raiders. Entering a squadron is much like going into a college fraternity; new people had to be tested—if you were rated third class and above they were, were your bosses (The Navy Way) would do several jobs, anything but electronics.

The Korean War broke out on June 25; North Korea attacked South Korea. The base was secured so anyone on leave was called back to the base. All hands including Junior Officers were put to work belting ammunition. All five squadrons started intense flying. We went on the Carrier US Midway to qualify pilots. One poor ensign had trouble getting into the correct position to land. After his last miss, the gun crews on the 40 mm yelled in unison, "Let us shoot him down." He must have heard the comment because he landed okay, still alive (The Navy Way).

Air Group #2 and CVG #6 split. Though we were VF-64, we were now in Air Group #2. We started planning to leave Oceania and go by troop train to the West Coast. Our planes flew ahead of us to San Diego. We had one officer in charge of us, Ensign Art Simmerly, we played cards day and night with plenty of beer brought aboard. Dinners were served by waiters; we used an old-fashioned laundry tub for hauling beer and ice. It took seven days as we were sidelined by faster trains.

We had to calculate "dry states" like Kansas and buy beer. One officer was in charge. Later at a CVG reunion: "Art, how did you like our trip across country?"

The Officer replied, "I never had so much fun!"

Bill Crouse at Boot Camp, Great Lakes, Illinois

The Yokuska Beer Hall—"Our Home Away
from Home!"—December 1950

Wakiki Beach—Diamond Head in the Background

A Supply Ship—Bring on the Bombs and Other Supplies

After a Mission Planes Landing with Only
Seconds of Separation Between Planes

Plane has all the Hydraulics Shot Out - 20 mm.
Canon Shot Off., Hit the Sailor to my left, His Foot
had to be removed. - A Close Call for Me

Back in the USA, Going under the Golden Gate Bridge
We were concerned the atenna woulg hit the Bridge!

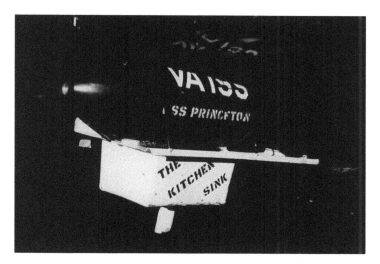

Air Group #19 Dropping the Kitchen Sink on
the Enemy, Sink on a 500 Lb. Bomb

Japanesse Shoe Shine Boy - Cost: 30 Yen

We landed in San Diego and went aboard the USS *Boxer*. Leading Chief on the morning of departure, "I can't tell you where we are going, but I think you know where." We left port and immediately got ground swells, waves about fifteen feet high for two hours. If you are going to get sick, this may do it, but few did. Being new to the squadron, I was placed on a fifty-caliber belting team from 7:00 PM to 7:00 AM, seven days a week. Our goal was one million rounds of fifty-caliber ammunition before our first operation. The irony of this, all was shot off in only three months of operation. Another fact, in only seven months of operation, we surpassed any WWII Carrier in ammunition shot off our ship.

We landed in Hawaii, picked up a pilot to navigate the narrow channel. The waterway to Ford Island was full of serpentine turns. Our ship was 880 feet long and could not turn fast enough. Solution: take thirty-two planes and put eight on stern and eight on portside. Place equal number on the starboard. To turn to the left (portside), the anchored planes would turn up full power and the carrier would gradually turn. When in position, all engines would stop until another turn was needed. The noise was hard on our ears.

Hawaii was a paradise. Temperatures would range from seventy-five to eighty-five degrees Fahrenheit, gentle breezes, palm trees, good food, and dancing girls wearing grass skirts.

I had a few drinks with one of my shipmates and headed back to the ship. We bumped into our squadron member Louis Hull, dead drunk hanging onto a lamp post. "Let's bring him back so he won't miss the eleven o'clock curfew." Carrying Louis with his heels dragging on the pavement about one-fourth of a mile was a task. Back at the carrier gang plank, Louis woke up and took off back to town. "At least we tried, let him go!" At morning muster, to our surprise, Louis was there. "Louis, what happened to the heels of your shoes? Look at that. Someone cut a forty-five-degree angle on your heels!"

We landed at Ford Island, Hawaii, for a little liberty (we were only there for three or four days). We saw the sunken Arizona, it was not a visitor's monument at that time. We then loaded up with supplies plus about five hundred marines. They slept on cots on the hangar deck; tough as marines are, some were sick (land lubbers) (The

Navy Way). Still belting fifty caliber, landed in Saseso, Japan. Some distance off Japan, we could detect an oriental smell. Off with the marines, two days to resupply. It took a day or so to have the pilots fly; had got them ready. Japanese are all about a foot shorter than us; how come they fought so hard? Received our first "dear John" from Peggy McMan. First action was Inchon invasion on September 15 till 1950. Two of us passed up a box of fifty-caliber ammunition out to the deck edge, and what are all those small boats LCT, LSO, LST doing circling near us. They were headed to Wolmida Island. A plane took off and crashed on the port (left side) and caused a fire. In a crash like this, the screws (propeller) were to stop so as not to chop up the pilot. Saw the pilot in the water on the edge of the flames. First thought: any loose powder and we may end the war now. Man up; this is insane. The pilot was burned on hands and about the face. He was flying again in about a week. Another note: On a fiftieth anniversary of war, I met a destroyer captain, one of three destroyers called "sitting ducks" who the day before the invasion destroyed any guns on Wome-Do Island, one destroyer was hit. Good job (The Navy Way).

Task force #77 consisted of two or three carriers on the battleship Missouri or a cruiser and about twelve or fifteen destroyers, a mighty, powerful force. About seven to eight ships would leave the task force to shell if needed off Korea. The battleships could fire sixteen-inch shells twenty miles—wow!

We are still belting ammo hard below the flight deck as the operation goes on above—noise, noise. Cousairs have two thousand horsepower engines. Before starting the engine, the propellers were turned over for about five minutes to get the oil out of the bottom of the engine. Every third day a supply ship would pull us along the starboard (right side) of the carrier to bring more supplies. We were out of ammunition. The rough weather was a sight to see—like two bobbing corks. I was tapped to work parties. Five-hundred-pound and one-thousand-pound bombs could be moved with ease. They were placed on a "dolly" with brackets to move right and left broke off (off it goes). When the ship rolls to a stop, wait for the movements your way (The Navy Way). The hangar was decked with work parties when no PO (petty officer) was looking and a case or two would go down the hatch—a mixture of fruit cocktails, lemon, alcohol (stolen from the medical department). Several jugs of the "hooch" were placed in the overhead ventilators (shades of captain Quig in the book *Mr. Roberts*). The warm air would start the fermentation. After two or three weeks "party time"! What if an Officer or Master of Arms found out? At the time, our compartment smelled like a brewery. To hell with it; take a chance! (The Navy Way.)

Every once in a while, Bill Lumpp and I would escape from a work party, and we would hide in a secret place on the starboard side of the ship and look over the whole refueling and rearming operation. If the smoking lamp was lit, we could smoke cigarettes up there. We could not smoke if gas or fumes were present. Packs of cigarettes cost ten cents per pack or $1 per carton. At this price, many smoked. As the supply ship crossed close to our "birds nest," we would bet if the large Portuguese man of war would be sliced in two by the sharp bow of the supply ship. Sometimes I would win or lose a small monetary bet.

Our large carrier had three large engines. A speed of twenty knots had to be across the flight deck to launch planes. Jets were catapulted off because of their slow start. To see a catapult is like watching a perfectly choreographed dance. Precision, precision, precision (The Navy Way).

Our troops were advancing to the 38th parallel, the war may be over; home for Christmas? Because we had lost one engine, we would be going home. We stopped at Alamedia, California, then to NAAS Santa Rosa. Some were given leave, but I stayed behind. Not much pressing work to do. We did some flying as pilots had gotten some flight time in each month.

In early December, the Chinese Hords crossed the 38th parallel and a new more intense war started. We were activated again and we were headed to San Diego and boarded the Valley Forge (called the Happy Valley). All leaves were cancelled. This is amazing; people were scattered all over the USA, yet no one missed our departure (The Navy Way).

It is now winter off Korea, and it was the coldest in several years. Sometimes operations were halted because of heavy snowstorms; I was working the flight deck for the next four months. To work, I wore long johns, a sweater with heavy foot weather gear, plus a helmet and goggles, topped off with "flight deck shoes." They had hoses on the bottom of the shoe—like small suction cups. I had heavy gloves plus hot coffee (the Navy Way).

In Airman Preliminary School, they taught us how to handle a prop wash over 100 mph. Metal strips crossed the deck about every six feet. All planes had to run their engines at full power before take-off. The plane captains were subject to this danger on all take offs. They had to remove the chocks on each wheel before the plane could move. We could not lift our head with the danger of getting blown down the deck into the other planes.

One time, I was caught in this situation. VF-64 plane had radio trouble, so I responded after the wind died down. I tried everything but no contact with the tower. So I gave thumbs down and the combat mission was cancelled. The plane was pulled and went down to the hangar deck for repairs. I am an airman (the same as a corporal in the army) downing a plane. That is quite a bit of responsibility; maybe I should get more money? A corsair in a full power take off, the plane had to be given full right rudder to prevent a torque roll. The pilots were sometimes killed in this type of crash.

On a payday, I counted twenty-one poker games throughout the Happy Valley. On the upper level over the hangar deck a Chief Petty Officer had a poker game that took $1,000 to enter. A guy was posted outside with his hand on a light switch. If an officer or shore patrol showed up, light would go out—all evidence was hidden in minutes. (Yes, it was the Happy Valley, not much discipline; we love it.) (The Navy Way.)

As the weather warmed up, we crossed down the China Coast to photo the coast line. The Chinese were shelling Iwo Island close to Formosa, Komoy, and Matsu. Tried to let them know we are in the area (The Navy Way).

We had to swap ships' planes from the Carrier Happy Valley to the USS *Philippine Sea*; crews swapped ashore, planes at sea. We had their planes so it was natural that we painted bad things on their planes before takeoff. I never heard of such swear words and sexual pictures. Winds gusting to 20 to 30 mph; this should be great to watch, counting I saw twenty-one wrecks trying to land. No pilot was lost, but our fine planes were a mess—a mechanic's nightmare.

We had a squadron of night fighters, probably about four planes. They would fly off just at dusk and spend three to four hours over Korea. The pilot and two radar operators really had guts to fly at night. Landing was the real problem. The carriers were dark with the exception of one light visible for five miles. At night, distances cannot be perceived because there is no reference to any land markers. Just before landing the LSO (landing signal officer) would switch on the deck lights. There were fewer accidents, but they do happen.

One day, I was below deck, and I reached for the heavy steel hatch door at the same time a guy slammed it on my finger, crushing the three longest finger nails. All black, excess pain—off to sick bay. A corpsman with a drill drilled the top of three nails as blood gushed out—but pain gone. Why me?

Someone once asked, "Did you have the atom bomb on your ship?" I don't think we did, but the AD Skybender probably could have carried the bomb called "Little Boy."

We were paid with MPC (military pay certificates). All would buy Japanese yen for 360 yen for one US dollar. For example, a fifth of Canadian Club Whiskey cost just a little over $3. There are lots of bargains, and we were their best customers.

We stopped at Hawaii again where the weather was great. It rained about one-half hour each day. Had a few hours off so we went to the Royal Hawaii Revolving Bar where drinking one too many; got off the seat and could not find my seat. "Someone has been moving the seats." A Samaritan guided me to my empty seat. It is time to go back to the ship. Our planes frequently had to "ditch" (go into the water). A water landing was very dangerous if a plane flipped upside down. One plane skipped like a stone on the water and the pilot unbuckled his safety harness and jumped out on the wing. A rescue helicopter picked him up; his shoes were still dry. Another pilot— not so lucky—he was completely soaked. The helicopter picked him up as soon as he was safe; he came up to the radio shack and one of our group had 180 proof alcohol; dip watch for five minutes then blow it out. Pilot safe, back working, all is well (The Navy Way.)

My original enlistment was three years but President Truman added another year. At the same time, we were given the GI bill. The commander of all United Nations force, Matthew Bidgeway, paid us a visit. In a short speech, he said, "You're doing a great job, keep up the maximum effort." Poker was the more common game, however; a reservist Duncan McDonald invented a football game. Soon after, we were divided up in teams and we had "playoffs" just like it was at home.

The Jack London's Bar was located in Oakland, California. It was a very small bar, but the wall and ceiling was covered with signed one dollar bills. They requested that after serving in the Pacific wars, you come back and get your money—many did not make it; I still have a note at the bar.

In the winter of 1950–1951, we were back at our home base Yoksuka for replenishment. At the same time, the marines who walked back from the Chozen Reservoir were a mess with frostbite (their arms and legs were black). They were turned loose and alcohol was now taking command of their brains. They saw three or four sailors. They wanted to fight. Our response: "We don't fight cripples." The marine did not know that we (air group) cover their exit from Chozen Reservoir (The Navy Way).

We encountered three typhoons—Karen, Mary (unknown) with winds of a steady 75 mph with gusts over 100 mph. The flight deck was fifty feet off the water, yet waves were covering 25 percent of the forward deck. At the same time, the stern would move up out of the water to expose the propellers. All engines had to be stopped to save them from too many revolutions. I looked down the hangar deck and it would bend at separation plates. The top of waves were blown off so it was a constant sheet of rain. Where is my life jacket?

While working in the kitchen during General Quarters, I was placed as fourth loader on the twin 40 MM. My job was to pass the ammunition. The gun was about sixteen feet out on side of the ship. When firing, the vibration was bad. My wallet would shake out of my pocket; must carry a safety pin to secure it, had to keep cotton for my ears. I'm an electronic technician scrubbing dishes and now playing gunner on the forties (The Navy Way).

In bad sections of the country, we would roll a tube of dimes in our kerchief and tie them down. It makes a great club—never had to use the weapon—be prepared (the Navy Way).

After thirty-nine months, I was discharged and returned home. Someone asked, "How is the chow (food)?" Answer: I was 175 pounds; at home, weight was 149! I still won't eat beans, fruit cocktail, or green scrambled eggs.

Went to Hawaii five times, crossed the international date line three times, awarded "Golden Dragon." Never cross the Equator, one way to lose a day in time; the other way, you have two days the same?

When taking showers on ship, rules: one-minute saltwater, soap up, then one minute with fresh water. The Master of Arms enforced the rules. The toilets were just a trough of running salt water with about five seats. Saw the high man, lighted some toilet paper, and set it loose floating downhill—called the hot seat (ouch).

Boarded the USS *Philippine Sea* with the rest of the CY#2s. After watching the twenty-one crashes those of us were sent to work as "mess cooks." Our job was to work in the scullery wrestling dishes. This duty is like slavery; working fifteen hours a day with only an hour off afterward from three until four to relax. Here I am an electronics technician; so far, I belted fifty-caliber compartment cleaner, was fourth loader on gun turret, worked most loading ammunition and food. For twelve hours at night, I made five-inch rockets. I was issued a hammock, which was put away in the workday. Hammocks are great—no ships rock and roll. I was half awake when a thief lifted my wallet. My pants were hung up on the end of my hammock; I was only in my underwear and T-shirt, and I chased the thief up two decks, but I lost him and was now very mad. The next day, the master at arms found my wallet. Money gone but there was only $2 in it. All IDs and identification were intact. It is hard to replace all military cards, etc. We started back to the States, landing at Alameda then back to Santa Rosa. While going into port, we had to stand at formation. I hope our large antenna missed the low point of the

Golden State Bridge. The band would play the National Anthem of all nations. Some like Japanese were really weird sounding.

On one of the ships in winter operations, a man fell overboard into freezing water. He was only given ten minutes before hypothermia took over. The ship dropped a lighted buoy. Somehow he swam to the light and he hugged the buoy—then fainted. The rescue ship picked him up—what a lucky guy. He survived. In port, in Japan, a sailor missed morning muster due to too much alcohol; he fell off the fantail (stern). His body floated up and it had several crabs trying to eat him—not a nice way to die.

Just as a precaution, General Quarters was sounded every morning and evening. We were only once or maybe twice fired on by shore batteries. Shells all fell short; we just turned tail.

As I was on the USS *Princeton*, my old ship, USS *Boxer* with my old Air Group #2 had a near disaster. On the hangar deck, a fifty-caliber gun went off and hit a gas tank on another plane. Fire went to the other aircraft. A five-hundred-pound bomb exploded and the fire magnified. I was in port as the ship (fire now out) came into port. I paid them a visit—what a mess. Some died and many were injured or burned. Some had to jump overboard rather than get burned. They say the Air Group with their firefighting saved the ship; it was listing fifteen degrees.

At one time, the ship was searched for drugs coming into the USA by the Federals. No one could leave until the search was completed; it took about two hours (none were found).

Several times, I saw sailors after leaving the ship get off and kiss the ground. At the same time, most ships held an anchor pools. Some had large amounts of money for first prize. They would announce the exact time. Each side of the pool had winners. I once won $25 by hitting the side of a pool.

Now with VA-195, we were moved to Moffit Field, California about sixty miles south of San Francisco. The hangars were about three hundred feet or more in height. They had their own atmosphere. It was sunny outside, but it rained with a fine wet mist. Everyone went on vacation, so for two months, I didn't do much—cards, handball, basketball. I was only three months from getting discharged; working on the Skyraider was great—no armor to move and you worked standing up. Upon arriving in Moffit Field, I tried to call home on a pay phone (I put in ten cents and nothing worked). I asked someone, "Try putting in twenty-five cents." Boy, I felt stupid.

The food (chow) at Moffit Field was excellent. They even had a weekend brunch for those who wanted to sleep in. We learned later that the Chief Commissary was taking food from us and selling them in Santa Rosa. He was later charged with a crime. Hope they put him on bread and water. My normal weight was 175 lbs. Mother's cooking was the answer. As of now, I won't wait in lines as I can't stand baked beans, fruit cocktail, or green scrambled eggs.

Now with a skeleton crew at Moffit Field, we had much time on our hands. The boys wanted to play basketball. I'm not a good ball player but it will kill some time.

Remember, I worked in a family store during WWII; did not play in sports. Played basketball one day and made a few points. One of the men on our team was an officer. He said, "I looked at your record, if you pack your gear, I'll send you to Treasure Island" (the local discharge center). I moved fast and packed up my sea bag. In Treasure Island, we could look over and see Alcatraz Prison. While there, FASRON #8 wanted to hire me for $5 per hour working on electronic gear. I declined the offer and left with almost $1,000 on me. Mustering out pay was used for leave and food rations; I'm gone, heading East.

Air Group #2 had quite a record:

(1) Time overseas, nineteen months total
(2) Three tours of Korea: 1950–1952
(3) In the four months shot off one million rounds of fifty-caliber ammunition. I loaded some of those shells.
(4) In four months, we shot off more ammunition than any other carrier in WWII
(5) Longest time at sea, forty-two days.
(6) Set the speed record from Japan CVG to California (a little over four days)

(7) Air Group #2 was the most decorated Naval Air Group of the Korean War. They were awarded the Navy Unit Citation Ribbon

(8) During rough weather in the ship's bow, we had to tie ropes on three sides of our rack (bunk) and climb in this open end; otherwise, we could get ejected from our bunk.

(9) North Korea would drop mines in the waters and they would drift toward us in TF #77. Minesweepers would try to eliminate the danger. One night one hit one of our destroyers. Two of the crew was KIA and several of the crew was wounded. In bunk in the bow, I could hear the waves hitting the sides of the carrier. Since I had no control of the mines, let's not worry and get some sleep.

(10) For entertainment, we placed marbles on steel deck. They would roll and hit with a loud bang as they hit the steel bulk head (edge). The phone rings: "This is Commander (so and so) I'm trying to sleep. Stop that noise or you will all be in the brig (jail)." Tales of the book *Mr. Roberts*.

(11) Early in the war, by mistake, we shot down a two-engine British plane. The pilot and crew died and were placed in our cold storage. No one would talk about this incident (The Navy Way).

(12) All pilots had to qualify by getting proficient in carrier landings. This is called a shakedown cruise. Practice makes perfect. One new pilot made several passes and the LSO (landing signal officer) gave him all "wave offs." Our LSO Tobias was held in very high esteem. His responsibility was awesome. After several tries landing the gun crew in unison started yelling "Shoot him down." At the same time, a plane landed on one of our planes and chopped up the cockpit. I picked up Ensign Gaffner's helmet. Inside was the top half of the poor pilot's head; I saw gray matter with very little blood. "Bill, why are you not going to chow?" "No, my stomach is for some reason not in need of food now."

I had a good Kodak S28 camera, so I took lots of pictures and often exposed myself to dangerous situations. Our attitude: "We're too young to die" (The Navy Way).

Learned of a plan coming in with loss of all hydraulics (shot up), no wheels down, and no flaps down, so I grabbed my camera and took pictures as the plane crashed. The 50-mm cannon fired one shot. It hit the man on deck just to my left. Doctors took off his foot above the ankle. If I would have moved twelve degrees to the left, it would have hit me in the head—another close one.

I had no pictures of jets taking off; remember, I had a green shirt, so I could go where the action was (flight deck). I got in position for a good shot; the jet turned but the barrier to stop the blast was still down. The slip stream hit me full force, lifted me off my feet, and I was headed to the side of the ship. Luckily, my feet caught the metal fence and stopped me from going over the side; maybe I'm indestructible?

While in port (Yoksuka), we hired a group of Japanese workers to do some maintenance on the hangar deck. It would be a good chance to see how the natives using chopsticks picked up cooked rice and tuna fish. A big bowl of lunch was placed before about twenty workers. Each one had their own finger bowl and chopsticks. Into their bowls went a big scoop of rice. I was watching closely as the bowls went to their mouth, then the chopsticks were like a shove, what a disappointment. I do know now that sticky rice will adhere to chopsticks.

Our Chief Petty Officers were products of the carrier wars in the South Pacific. Some were close to retirement and each department like, metal, electronics; ammunition mechanics had a chief or at least a First-Class Petty Officer. They ran the squadron and they were excellent.

The Officer in charge of electronics was Ensign Smith. He knew nothing about electronics; each officer in addition to being a pilot was given an assignment. He would show up about once a month in the radio room: "You men are doing a good job, keep it up" (The Navy Way).

Back in Santa Rosa, California, the squadron was given money for the men to get bats and balls and other athletic equipment. Word passed to us it would be put to a vote: buy athletic equipment or have a party at Leana's (local watering hole). I think you know the winner: "party time!" And the party was a success—great food, free booze. Just before leaving, we notice Ensign Smith completely unconscious in the corner of the bar. "Let's bring him back. Put him in the back seat of his convertible." We tried to hassle him so we could get past the guard. The guard seeing a wings like noting an Officer; he saluted us and we saluted back. Then we found his room at the BOQ (bachelor officer quarters). We didn't get in until like perhaps two or three o'clock. Saturday, at 8:00 AM, we had to fall in for muster. Ensign Smith was doing fine, yet all of us were tired. Conclusion: VF#64 was made up of men—"made of steel."

Question: how does your aircraft find the carriers with thousands of miles of open ocean? In a little box, the size of a shoebox housed the ZB. This is not what the technical name for the ZB. But is what we called them. All aircraft had one and it had to be on frequencies in all planes. In a 360-degree circle was divided up with twenty-four sections at fifteen-degree difference. As a pilot would pick up a radio signal in Morse Code from the ship, he would look at a chart and it would tell him to turn to a heading of, for example, 110 degrees. The signal only was unidirectional but would widen as it distanced from the source. By following the signal, it would always lead him until he had a visual of the TE #77. The ships radar could help in looking for a landing.

In Santa Rosa, on Sunday morning, we found a church with one of my shipmates decided to go to church. This was a small church, outside was a sign that stated this whole church was made with one redwood tree. It probably had the capacity of about one hundred to five hundred parishioners. After services, a parishioner with his family invited us to go to dinner at his house. We were in uniform and he explained that he was at Pearl Harbor at the beginning of the Japanese attack. He was an officer on the Arizona. But that day, Sunday morning, he was lucky to be ashore. People like this are what make Santa Rosa a great little village. Getting ready to leave, our host stated that "Divers were sent into the sunken Arizona to remove dead bodies of those trapped below." However, in the searching of officers' quarters, they found a package with our hosts name on it and returned it to him. My host said, "Sailors, you have had the privilege of eating dinner on a piece of history. China servings from the sunken Arizona."

While on the 40-mm gun, we would practice firing every once in a while. A plane would pull over a sleeve and we would shoot at it. Those flying had a lot of guts to let us shoot at this sleeve. The battle ship *Missouri* was now to shoot all of their 5" 38's guns – and they cut loose with all guns blazing. They missed the sleeve but a destroyer fired three out of three times. Bingo, they hit the target. The small destroyers blew their whistles. I could hear the gun crews yelling over their victory.

MEMBERS OF AIR GROUP #19
– FOREVER HEROS
MIA/KIA/POW

Death into Life, War into Peace, Hate into Love. For these ends our courageous have died. It was their hope to reap a peaceful solution from the Korean police action. That their sacrifice has not been in vain, that the world someday can enjoy freedom from war . . . this book is dedicated.

Ralph Cross, LTJG, USNR
Glynn Francis Dutemple, LCDR, USN
Sammy Edward Erwin, SN, USN
Richard Eugene Garver, LT, USN
Charles Rutherford Holman, LTJG, USN
Robert Jay Humphrey, LT, USNR
Richard Loran Jackson, LT, USNR
William Ellis Pulliam II, LT, USN
James Sherman Rife, AN, USN
Adler Earl Ruddell, AT3, USN
Forest Dean Swisher, ENS, USN
Durward Jerome Tennyson, LT, USN
Howard Wilson Westervelt, LTJG, USN
Owen Foch Williams, LT, USNR

In Remembrance of Them . . .

MEMBERS OF AIR GROUP #2 – FOREVER HEROS
MIA/KIA/POW

THE FINAL FORMATION FOR THESE OFFICERS AND MEN OF CARRIER AIR GROUP TWO (CVG-2) WAS MADE DURING THE KOREAN CONFLICT AND THE KNOWLEDGE THEY MAY BE CALLED UPON TO MAKE THE SUPREME SACRIFICE FOR THE UNITED STATES OF AMERICA . . . EACH OF THEM IN THE HIGHEST TRADITIONS OF THE UNITED STATES NAVY PROUDLY AND SELFLESSLY GAVE THE LAST BREATH OF THEIR LIVES TO SERVE OUR COUNTRY.

FINAL INFORMATION
(Korean War)
MIA/KIA/POW

BALL, WILLIAM R., LT(JG), VF-63
BREY, ELWOOD E., ENSIGN, VA-65
BRINKLEY, JOHN, ENSIGN, VF-63
BURDETTE, WILLIAM B., ATAN, VC-35
CANALES, IGNACIO, JR., AN, VA-65
CONKLIN, RAYMOND, LCDR, VF-24
COWGER, VERNON L., PN3, VF-64
DICK, JAMES B., LT (JG), VF-64
GRIFFITH, JACK W., LT., CAG.
GUSSNER, JOHN G., ENSIGN, VF-24
HOWELL, CLAUDE C., ENSIGN, VF-24
KOFFMAN, EMORY R., LCDR, VF-24
KORDELESKI, JOHN E., LT (JG), VF-64
LOOMMER, RICHARDS C., ENSIGN, VF-24
MARTIN, GEORGE A., ENSIGN, VF-24
MC COSKRIE, DAVID L., LT (JG), VC-3
MESSERSCHMIDT, RICHARD C., LT (JG) VA-64

MOLLER, EUGENE H., ENSIGN, VF-63
MURPHY, RAYMOND, ENSIGN, VF-64
NEEL, WALTER P., KCDR, VA-65
RICHTER, EDWARD J., ENSIGN, VA-65
ROWE, RICHARD C., LT(JG), VA-65
SEAMAN, CLIFFORD, LT (JG0, VA-65
SHROPSHIRE, JAMES S., LT, CAG
SMITH, FRANKLIN, LT (JG), VF-63
SODEN, FRANKLIN, LT(JG), VF-63
SODEN, BILLY G., AT2, VC-35
TAYLOR, RICHARD S., HN, VF-24
TUTHILL, MAURICE A., ENSIGN, VF-64
TWINKLE, AUSTIN J., LT, VF-24
WARK, JAMES C., HN3, VF-64
WEST, CLARENCE E., ENSIGN, VF-63

LT. OBBORNE (VF-63), LT (JG) DEMASTERS (VF-64), AND ENSIGN FALER (VA-65) WERE RELEASED DURING POW EXCHANGES AT PANMUNJON, THOUGH REPORTED MAI/KIA IN EARLIER REPORTS.

**THIS INFORMATION WAS OBTAINED AT A
CARRIER AIR GROUP TWO REUNION**

9 781644 168431